The 6 Phases of Building Wealth

The Step-By-Step Guide to Achieving Financial Freedom

Trevor E. Griffin, R. Phill Hampton, Jr., and
Geoffrey F. Vibert

ISBN-13: 978-1974441013
ISBN-10: 1974441016

To our family and friends

Contents

Foreword

"Money makes the world go round". This phrase can be traced back to the mid-20th century and yet, it is still so true today. In our world, those who have money are free to shape their lives as they see fit, while the less fortunate among us toil away, struggling to make ends meet. At least this is how my friends and I saw it in the early 2000s, while complaining to each other one day on our lunch break. We were three guys who had lucked out in life in many ways. Born in America (a much-underappreciated advantage), to families approaching middle class, we had each graduated from college with a bachelor's degree, and were now working "good" jobs. Each of us had solid familial support systems behind us. By almost any measure, we were successful. And yet, we did not feel that way. So what was it we were missing? After some thoughtful reflection, we determined the answer was **Financial Freedom**.

From the outside, we may have been perceived as three successful men, living the "American dream", but the reality was much different. Bills, debt, insufficient savings, and limited investments. These were the things that made up our financial picture. We realized, if we did not take action to change our situation, we would be facing a lifetime of work, capped off by a short retirement, potentially spent living in poverty. With this bleak picture in our minds, we decided to form a business together. The sole purpose of this business would be to pursue methods of achieving Financial Freedom. As we worked toward this goal, we encountered a multitude of strategies for budgeting, saving, eliminating debt, and investing. Over time, we began to recognize that the vast majority of the tools and resources needed to achieve Financial Freedom were available to common, everyday people. This discovery motivated us to continue our search. Over the years, we identified the strategies we felt were most effective and eliminated the ones that were not as useful. We began to formulate a step-by-step system for achieving Financial Freedom. As we implemented this system in our own lives, and started to enjoy some success, we decided to share the strategies we had discovered with our closest friends and family members. We began creating a document, which briefly summarized the simple techniques we had developed. As the contents of the document grew, we realized, with a little extra work, this "document" had the potential to become a full-fledged book. And so, we turned it into just that!

It should be noted that we are not professional financial advisors or planners. We are not bankers or stockbrokers. In fact, we have no official training in the financial industry whatsoever. We are simply three guys who decided we wanted a brighter financial future for our families and ourselves and thus, we set out on a journey of discovery. After nearly a decade of trial and error, hits and misses, and experimentation and research, we believe we have developed a system that can help almost anyone achieve Financial Freedom.

The system—and by extension—this book, consists of six "phases". The focus of each phase is to complete a specific financial goal. The phases are designed to be completed in order, one after the other. Following each phase is an on-going case study, which provides specific implementation examples. In each case study, you will follow "David" as he works toward Financial Freedom. Before attempting to implement any of the recommendations contained within this book, we advise it be read in its entirety. This will give a clearer view of the overall goal and the nature of the methods used to achieve it. Now, let's get started!

PHASE 1

Budgeting

The first, and perhaps most important step in your journey to Financial Freedom is to construct a detailed monthly budget. A monthly budget, done properly, will give you a clear picture of how every dollar you make is being utilized each month. Once created, you will continually update and consult your budget. It will be the primary document you use to track your progress along the way. If you have never created a budget it may feel like a very intimidating process. However, the budgeting system we recommend is easy to follow and can be implemented quickly. It is called the "50/20/30" budget. This system requires that you build your budget based on the following three spending categories:

❖ 50% Fixed Expenses – This category consists of all of your fixed living expenses. Bills that are necessary/unavoidable such as housing costs, utility payments, prescription purchases, transportation costs, health insurance payments, minimum debt payments, and grocery bills are examples of fixed expenses.

❖ 20% Wealth-Building - This category consists of money that will be used to build wealth and achieve financial goals. This includes paying off debt, investing, and saving.

❖ 30% Flexible Spending - The final category consists of non-essential/flexible spending. This includes things like cable TV, eating out, gym memberships, vacations, and shopping.

The number assigned to each category represents the percentage of your **after-tax income** that should be allocated to it. In other words, no more than 50% of your after-tax income should go towards Fixed Expenses; no more than 30% should go toward Flexible Expenses; and no less than 20% should go towards Wealth-Building. Use the following steps to get your 50/20/30 budget started.

Step 1

Compile your pay stubs and determine how much after-tax money you are bringing home each month. If you have money being automatically deducted for health insurance and/or retirement savings, be sure to include it as part of this total. Also include any additional regularly occurring income you may have from other sources.

Step 2

Create your initial budget by recording all of your monthly bills, expenses, savings, and investments in a spreadsheet, text document, or on a piece of paper. You should be able to access these numbers by reviewing your bank and credit card statements. If you have trouble finding all of the information you need, do not attempt to estimate your expenses. An inaccurate estimate could ruin your budget. Instead, you will need to spend some time collecting data. Begin tracking and recording all of your daily expenditures. Expenses may fluctuate from month to month, so continue to capture this data for 60-90 days to formulate a monthly average. This will enable you to determine your total monthly expenses. Alternatively, you can also track expenses using financial websites or software (see *Additional Information* for a list of recommended budgeting tools).

Step 3

Organize each item in your budget into one of the three spending categories (Fixed, Flexible, or Wealth-Building). Every single dollar spent should be marked as either a fixed or flexible expense. Every single dollar saved or invested should be marked as a Wealth-Building expenditure.

> **Note:** The minimum monthly payment amount of any debt you have is considered a fixed expense and should be marked as such. Any funds you were previously using to pay debt, that go above the minimum monthly payment, should be reallocated to the Wealth-Building category. For now, you should only be making the minimum required payments on all debts. In *Phase 3: Debt Elimination*, we will provide additional details regarding how and when to increase your monthly debt payments.

Step 4

After organizing your expenses, if you find you are already meeting the parameters of a 50/20/30 budget, congratulations! You are on the path to Financial Freedom, and may now move on to *Phase 2: The First $1,000.* For those whose spending habits don't yet meet the criteria of a 50/20/30 budget, there may be some difficult challenges ahead. You must begin the process of adjusting some of your views and habits as they relate to money. Completing this step may require some significant changes to your current lifestyle.

If you find that you are spending more than 50% of your income on fixed expenses, you must take steps to lower those expenses. If your rent or mortgage payment is too high, you may need to find a less expensive place to live. If your utility bills are too high, you should work on conserving energy by powering off lights when they are not in use, unplugging computers or other devices when they are not being charged, changing the thermostat settings, or using water more efficiently. If your car payment, insurance, or gasoline expenses are too high, you may want to consider getting a more cost-effective vehicle (e.g. more fuel-efficient, lower cost to insure, cheaper car, etc.), or occasionally walking/biking instead of driving. Making some of these changes is no small feat and can have a huge impact on the way you live, but you have to ask yourself, "Would I rather live in a big house/luxurious apartment or be able to retire at the age of 55 instead of 75? Is taking shorter showers and turning off the lights when I'm done with them too much to ask if it will help me financially? Does driving a fancy car give me more pleasure than watching my savings and investments grow?" Only you can answer these questions.

If you find that you are spending more than 30% of your income on flexible expenses, you must take whatever steps necessary to lower these expenses. This may mean scaling back the amount you spend on things like cable TV, eating out, and vacationing. You may need to limit your shopping habits or cut down on expensive hobbies. Again, these choices will not be easy to make, but you must put things into perspective and decide if these luxuries are more important to you than your Financial Freedom (e.g. is cable TV worth postponing your Financial Freedom?).

Once your spending habits have been adjusted to align with your 50/20/30 budget, any remaining income should be used for Wealth-Building. When your budget is fully implemented, 20% should be the MINIMUM you have allocated to the Wealth-Building category. Ideally, you'll be able to contribute even more than 20%. The more that you save and invest, the faster you will be able to achieve Financial Freedom. Since Financial Freedom is the goal of *The 6 Phases of Building Wealth*, you should dedicate as much money to the Wealth-Building category as possible.

Step 5

Your budget will be your guide throughout your financial journey. Keep it updated and refer to it often.

CASE STUDY 1

David is a 35-year-old contractor with a monthly, after-tax, household income of $3,000. He has put together a list of all of his expenditures and organized them into categories based on the 50/20/30 budget plan.

David's Initial Budget

Fixed Expenses		Wealth-Building		Flexible Expenses	
Rent	$1,000	Monthly Saving	$50	Eating Out	$350
Utilities	$150	Debt payments above minimum	$150	Entertainment	$150
Car Insurance	$100			Hobbies	$100
Groceries	$150			Gym	$50
Gasoline	$75			Cable TV	$150
Health Insurance	$150			Internet	$75
Minimum Debt Payments	$550			Mobile Phone	$120
				Subscriptions	$50
				Shopping	$200
Total	**$2,175**	**Total**	**$200**	**Total**	**$1,245**
% of Income	**72.5%**	**% of Income**	**6.7%**	**% of Income**	**41.5%**

Total	$3,620
% of Income	120.7%

Current Savings	$0

Table 1.1 David's Initial Budget

Note: Notice that in David's initial budget, his monthly expenditures are greater than his actual monthly income. This means each month he is accruing additional debt.

Over the course of a month, David analyzes his expenditures and determines that there are some areas where he can reduce his spending. He also finds there are some expenses he can eliminate entirely. In a relatively short time, he is able to make some lifestyle adjustments, which lower his expenses. He updates his budget accordingly.

David's Phase 1 Budget

Fixed Expenses		Wealth-Building		Flexible Expenses	
Rent (cheaper apartment)	$600	Saving, Investing, and Paying Debt	$600	Eating Out (more cooking)	$200
Utilities (more efficient use)	$75			Entertainment	$150
Car Insurance (increased deductible)	$75			Hobbies	$100
Groceries (bargain shopping)	$100			Gym	$50
Gasoline (walking/biking)	$50			Cable TV (discontinued)	$0
Health Insurance	$150			Internet	$75
Minimum Debt Payments	$550			Mobile Phone	$120
				Subscriptions	$50
				Shopping (no impulse buys)	$55
Total	$1,600	Total	$600	Total	$800
% of Income	53.3%	% of Income	20.0%	% of Income	26.7%

Total	$3,000
% of Income	100%

Current Savings	$0

Table 1.2 David's Phase 1 Budget

David's budget isn't perfect; his fixed expenses are still slightly over budget. However, the important thing is that he has become proactive in improving his financial well-being. As he continues along this path, things will only get brighter.

PHASE 2

The First $1,000

Now that you have your 50/20/30 budget implemented, it's time to begin saving! Your ultimate savings goal will be to have 6-12 months' worth of living expenses in your account, but we'll get to that later. Right now, your focus should be to save $1,000 as a starter emergency fund. A starter emergency fund acts as a cushion for any expenses that pop up unexpectedly as you go through the process of paying off debt in *Phase 3: Debt Elimination*. If you already have $1,000 or more saved, great! All you need to do in this phase is complete Step 1 and then you can move on to *Phase 3*. If you are starting your savings from scratch or haven't quite reached the $1,000 milestone, continue reading.

Step 1

Open a **high-yield savings account** to serve as your emergency fund. It is important that the account be a savings and not a checking account so that there are some built-in restraints on the speed and frequency with which you can access the cash. This will help you maintain spending discipline. Remember, this money should be used for emergencies only. All other spending should already be covered in your budget. It is also important that the account you open is high-yield. High-yield bank accounts offer a higher rate of return than a normal bank typically would. Many banking institutions that provide high-yield accounts forgo **brick-and-mortar** locations and operate online only to cut costs. They pass the savings on to their customers in the form of a higher rate of return. Conduct your own research online to identify which banks are currently offering the best rates on high-yield savings accounts and select one that best fits your needs (see *Additional Details* for a list of recommended banks).

Be sure to set up direct deposit or activate a recurring automatic bank transfer for every pay period so that the money you save will go directly into your new emergency fund. This money should automatically move to your emergency fund account before you can touch it. This may not seem like an important detail, but it is actually very significant. If the money is deposited into the account before you have any opportunity to interact with it, you will have a much easier time living as if it doesn't exist, and will be far less tempted to spend it.

Step 2

Saving $1,000 can seem like an unattainable goal for many, but it might not be as hard as you think. If you have successfully implemented your 50/20/30 budget (see *Phase 1: Budgeting*), then simply deposit the 20% you have designated to Wealth-Building into your emergency fund account each month, until you've reached $1,000. If you haven't quite perfected your budget or you're just itching to get to the next phase as swiftly as possible, we've included some additional steps below that will help you expedite reaching any savings goal.

Reduce spending

This is the most obvious way to increase your saving rate; the less you spend, the more you have available to save. Grab your budget sheet and take a look at the non-essential/flexible expenses. Determine what things you would be willing to cut back on. Perhaps you could rent a movie to watch at home instead of going out to the theater? Cook on a weekend instead of going out to eat? Bring leftovers to work instead of burning money (and gas) on restaurants/fast food? You may be surprised by the amount you end up saving just by making a few small changes. In addition, you might even develop some cost-effective habits that can be maintained indefinitely.

Work more

Working overtime is a great way to make extra money. If this option is available to you then go for it, and watch as you reach your goal in no time. If being paid to work overtime at your current place of business is not possible, then how about a part-time job? Money generated from working a few additional weekends per month or a few extra nights per week can quickly add up.

Increase your salary

Asking your manager or supervisor for a raise may seem like an outrageous request, but you might be surprised by the answer. If you are a valued employee and have shown you are a hard worker who is dedicated to getting things done, why shouldn't you receive a raise? Good employees are very difficult to find. Your manager may be willing to give you a bump in pay to keep you happy. If this does not work or you're not bold enough to make the request, another option would be to pursue learning/training opportunities offered at your job or an educational facility in your community. Depending on the offerings, you may be able to earn additional credentials, ranging from a certification or license, all the way to a full college degree. Many employers will even pay for you to pursue these opportunities. Once you've increased your qualifications you will be empowered with additional leverage when requesting a raise or applying for a promotion. You may even be able to acquire the skills needed to obtain a better, higher paying job.

Sell unneeded items

Look around your home. Examine the contents of drawers, cabinets, and closets. Look for old clothing that no longer fits your style preferences, old electronics that you've upgraded and no longer use, pieces of jewelry you don't wear, or books you have lying around. Find any items that are unwanted or unneeded. Just because you don't need these things doesn't mean someone else won't pay you cash for them. Create an account on an e-commerce website such as Craigslist.org, OfferUp.com, or eBay.com and list your items for sale. If you'd rather do things offline, you can host a garage sale or take your items to a pawnshop. Be sure to check listings online for similar items in order to help you determine how to price things.

Step 3

Bask in the glory of successfully achieving your first savings goal— your $1,000 emergency fund! Now put the memory of this account out of your mind. It is not to be touched (except in the case of an emergency).

CASE STUDY 2

With $0 saved in the bank, David is starting his emergency fund from scratch. He has $600 per month designated to Wealth-Building (see Table 1.2 David's Phase 1 Budget), but he would like even more. Toward that end, he schedules a meeting with his manager to discuss a raise. In the meeting, David emphasizes all of his great qualities as an employee and points out his high-performance ratings and willingness to go above and beyond to get the job done. His manager is impressed with the presentation and grants him a 4% raise in pay. This increases David's monthly income to $3,120, allowing him to raise his Wealth-Building allocation to $720 per month. With this increase, it only takes two months for David to save enough to complete his starter emergency fund!

Monthly Savings Record	
David's Initial Savings	$0
Savings After 1 Month	$720
Savings After 2 Months	**$1,440**

Table 2.1 David's Monthly Savings Record

David updates his budget with his new savings total.

David's Phase 2 Budget

Fixed Expenses		Wealth-Building		Flexible Expenses	
Rent	$600	Saving, Investing, and Paying Debt	$720	Eating Out	$200
Utilities	$75			Entertainment	$150
Car Insurance	$75			Hobbies	$100
Groceries	$100			Gym	$50
Gasoline	$50			Cable TV	$0
Health Insurance	$150			Internet	$75
Minimum Debt Payments	$550			Mobile Phone	$120
				Subscriptions	$50
				Shopping	$55
Total	$1,600	Total	$720	Total	$800
% of Income	51.3%	% of Income	23.1%	% of Income	25.6%

Total	$3,120
% of Income	100.0%

Current Savings	$1,440

Table 2.2 David's Phase 2 Budget

PHASE 3

Debt Elimination

For many of us, being in debt is just a part of life. Debt gives us the ability to easily purchase big-ticket items like cars and homes. It provides access to the funds necessary to pay for expensive colleges and universities. It even allows us to purchase everyday items like food and clothing. With debt, we can make all of these transactions while providing little to no up-front cash. In short, debt can be an extremely useful tool in helping us get the things we want. However, when you take on too much debt, it can have a disastrous effect on your finances. In order to become financially free, we must rid ourselves of debt, especially high-interest, **unsecured debt**, such as that of credit and charge cards. The following steps will guide you towards that goal.

> **Note:** Although the ultimate objective of this Phase is to be totally debt free, we do not consider paying off your mortgage as pressing an issue as wiping out other debt. Once all non-mortgage debt has been eliminated, feel free to move on to *Phase 4: Emergency Fund*.

Step 1

Take a look at your budget. All debt payments should be listed under the fixed expenses category as "minimum required debt payments" (or some similar label). As noted in *Phase 1: Budgeting*, at this point you should only be making the minimum required payment on any outstanding debt. That is about to change, as it is time to start eliminating your debt.

In a new document, or on a piece of paper, create four columns titled "Debt Name", "Amount Owed", "Interest Rate", "Minimum Payment" and "Creditor Contact Number". Make an entry in the table for each of your debts by entering the appropriate information into each of the columns you just created. You should be able to find the required information for each debt on the latest monthly statement you've received for it or online by logging into the associated account. If you can't find all the information you need, call the creditor directly and they will be able to provide any missing details.

Step 2

Once you've gathered all the information for each debt, find a comfy chair, pick up your phone, and get ready to make some calls. Your objective is to lower the interest rate on as many of your outstanding debts as possible. Many times, this can be achieved simply by asking. Going from oldest account to newest, call each creditor and request a lower interest rate. If the initial person you speak with doesn't have the authority to lower your interest rate, ask to speak to their supervisor. For the older accounts, emphasize how loyal you've been as a customer and express that you'd like to remain a customer into the future. Make sure to be polite, but also persistent. You should have a specific lower interest rate in mind that you feel would be acceptable. Before making your first call, spend some time doing research to develop an idea of what interest rates are currently available to someone in a similar financial situation to yours. You can do this by searching online for currently available credit offers and by reviewing offers you've received in the mail. If a creditor refuses to lower your rate, don't be discouraged. You'll be eliminating all of this debt in the very near future.

> **Note:** If the creditor of a **revolving line of credit** (e.g. credit cards, charge cards, home equity lines of credit, etc.) refuses to lower your interest rate, you should ask that the account be closed. Potentially losing a customer may motivate the creditor more than any other argument. If you're still not successful in getting a better rate, follow through with closing the account. You will still owe the remaining balance, but will have one less method of generating debt to worry about.

Sample negotiation scripts for reducing interest rates

* ❖ "Hello my name is _____, I'm a current customer and I'd like to speak to someone about lowering the interest rate on my credit card. Do you have the authority to help me with this?..."

* ❖ "I have been a loyal customer for __ years and I hope to remain a customer, however I feel my interest rate is too high and I would like to talk about lowering it to __%..."

❖ "It does not look like we will be able to come to an
   agreement. Unfortunately, I'm going to have to ask that my
   account be permanently closed..."

Step 3

Now that you've established exactly what you owe, there is a choice
to be made. We are going to highlight three different methods of
eliminating debt. Based on your current financial situation, personal
temperament, and personal preference, you will choose which
method is best for you.

Consolidation

The first method of paying off debt that we'll discuss is
Consolidation. This method consists of combining multiple debts into
one larger debt, preferably with a lower interest rate. This can be
accomplished in a variety of different ways; however, we will focus on
the following two:

❖ **Debt consolidation loan** - Seeking out additional debt to pay off
   existing debt may not seem like the best idea, but a debt
   consolidation loan can be a very helpful tool if utilized
   correctly. A debt consolidation loan is a personal loan taken out
   specifically to pay off existing debt. It allows you to combine all of
   your debts into one single lump sum, with one monthly payment
   and, ideally, a lower interest rate. You can secure a debt
   consolidation loan through your local bank or credit union or by

going through a company that specializes specifically in debt consolidation. If you are able to obtain favorable terms on your loan, this method can be one of the fastest and cheapest ways to get out of debt. It is not all good news however; there are some potential risks involved. Many consolidation loans require costly upfront **origination fees** that may be as high as 5% of the total loan amount. In addition, some loans charge penalties if you pay them off early, limiting your ability to get out of debt quickly. Last, any revolving lines of credit that you pay off with the loan will then be balance free and available for use. The temptation to fall back into old spending habits may be too much for some, potentially resulting in an even worse financial situation. For this reason, we recommend closing most, if not all, revolving credit accounts if you choose to consolidate your debt.

❖ **Credit card balance transfer** - Another way to consolidate debt is to transfer existing balances to a new credit card. Many banks will allow you to open a new account with a 0% **Annual Percentage Rate (APR)** for 12-24 months and a 0% balance transfer fee. This is the type of offer you should look for. You can find these special deals by contacting your local bank or by searching online. If you cannot get both 0% APR and a 0% balance transfer fee, this option becomes much less attractive. If there is a fee to make the transfer, paying off your debt could become much more expensive. In addition, it is very important that you never miss a payment and fully pay off your debt within the time frame allotted by the offer. If you fail to complete either of these, you may end up facing hefty fees and/or being charged additional interest.

Snowball

The Snowball method was developed to take advantage of the positive feelings that arise as you pay off individual debts one by one. The method is simple yet effective. Organize your debts from smallest to largest balance. Each month pay the minimum required on all debts except the smallest one. On the smallest debt, pay the maximum amount you can afford. Once you've totally paid off the smallest debt, begin attacking the second smallest debt by combining its minimum payment that you have already been paying, with the payment you were making on the original smallest debt. Once the second smallest debt is totally paid off, combine its payment with the minimum you are paying on the third smallest debt. Continue to build up the payment amount (i.e. minimum required payment + all payments from eliminated debts) as you move on to larger and larger debts. Do this until all debts are paid off. This method creates a sense of growing momentum as you quickly pay off smaller debts and continually increase the amount you put towards larger debts over time. Although it can be a more expensive way of eliminating debt when compared to others since the interest rate is not considered, many still choose this method. The sense of accomplishment it elicits, as debts are paid off, and the perception of increasingly building momentum keeps them motivated to complete the process.

High Interest First

This method is very similar to the Snowball approach, only instead of paying off debts based on their current balances, they are paid off according to their interest rates. Organize your debts from highest to lowest interest rate. Begin making minimum payments on all debts except for the one with the highest interest rate. On this debt, pay the maximum amount you can afford. Do this every month until the debt is paid off. Take the money you were using to pay the debt with the highest interest rate and add it to your payment on the debt with the next highest interest rate. Continue this process until all debts are paid off. This method may not provide the same positive emotional impact that the Snowball method offers, but it will save you both money and time. That is because, paying debts from highest to lowest interest rate is mathematically faster and cheaper than the Snowball method. You will pay less and accrue less interest because the high-interest debts are eliminated first.

Which method should you choose?

Consolidating your debts into one low or no interest balance is a great way to pay off debt. It has the potential to save you a significant amount of money if you can find a good offer. However, implementing this method requires a much more involved process than the others and the attractiveness of the offer depends a great deal on your ability to negotiate favorable terms on your consolidation loan. In addition, paying off, and thus freeing for use, all revolving lines of credit at once, risks putting you into a worse financial position than you started with if you're not disciplined.

The Snowball method of paying off debt is very popular. While it is, by far, the most emotionally satisfying method discussed here, it is also likely to be more expensive than some other options. By not considering the interest rates you will spend more money overall, but watching your debt disappear at a seemingly ever-accelerating rate can provide a great deal of visceral pleasure. Being able to quickly pay off some of your balances in full, while also increasing the payments on others, can have a huge positive psychological impact. Sometimes this is the type of motivation we need in order to stay focused on our objective.

While the High Interest First method may not achieve quite as large a savings as some consolidation techniques might, paying off debt from highest to lowest interest rate is still a very cost-effective technique. Furthermore, this method can be implemented instantly and provides motivation as you see your debts disappear one by one (though perhaps not as much motivation as the Snowball method). It also doesn't have the same time limitations that some consolidation methods come with. For these reasons, we recommend this method over the others.

With that being said, each method has its own pros and cons. All of these methods are vastly superior, in terms of time and cost, when compared to paying only debt minimums. You should analyze your personal situation, find your comfort zone, and decide which method (or combination of methods) is best for you.

Step 4

Review the Wealth-Building section of your budget. The funds allocated to this category will be used to pay off your debt. Immediately begin to implement the debt elimination strategy that you've selected. If you have chosen to use the Snowball or High Interest First method, record the starting payment amount for each debt in the document that you created in Step 1 (i.e. minimum payments for all debts except the one you are focusing on). Use this document to keep track of all your debts and the amount you are applying to each of them over time. If you have chosen to consolidate your debts, go to your local bank or credit union or search online to find a good consolidation offer. If you are unable to find a deal with favorable terms, you may want to consider selecting one of the other methods of debt elimination.

Step 5

Continue to follow your selected debt elimination strategy until all non-mortgage debts are paid off.

Note: You may have a desire to continue to save some money while paying off your debt. This is not a recommended strategy. For now, you should rely on your starter emergency fund to cover any emergency expenses that pop up unexpectedly. All other expenses should already be accounted for in your budget. The longer you hold debt, the more it will cost you in interest. Putting additional funds into your savings account instead of using them to pay down debt will literally cost you money.

CASE STUDY 3

David organizes all of his outstanding debts into the list below.

David's Debt Summary

Debt Name	Amount Owed	Interest Rate	Minimum Payment	Contact Number
Visa	$3,000	18.0%	$75	555-XXX-XXXX
MasterCard	$500	17.5%	$15	555-XXX-XXXX
Macys	$200	15.0%	$5	555-XXX-XXXX
Car Loan	$8,000	5.0%	$250	555-XXX-XXXX
Student Loan	$10,000	4.0%	$205	555-XXX-XXXX
Total	$21,700		$550	

Table 3.1 David's Debt Summary

Next, he consults his budget to determine the quantity of money currently allocated to Wealth-Building ($720—see Table 2.2 David's Phase 2 Budget). He takes this amount and adds it to the sum of all required minimum debt payments ($550) to compute the total amount that will be used to pay debt each month.

$$Total\ Monthly\ Debt\ Payment = \$720 + \$550 = \$1,270$$

Finally, David selects the debt elimination strategy that best fits him and begins paying off his debts.

Note: For simplification purposes, accrued interest is being ignored in the following examples.

Scenario A (Consolidation)

David chooses to consolidate his debts. He spends a few weeks doing research and is eventually able to find a good consolidation deal with no origination fees and an interest rate of 5%.

David uses the consolidation loan to pay off his outstanding debts. The balances are now all zero except for the new loan. His new debt summary can be seen below.

Consolidated Debt Summary

Debt Name	Amount Owed	Interest Rate	Minimum Payment
Consolidation Loan	$21,700	5%	$430
Visa	$0	18.0%	$0
MasterCard	$0	17.5%	$0
Macys	$0	15.0%	$0
Car Loan	$0	5.0%	$0
Student Loan	$0	4.0%	$0
Total	**$21,700**		**$430**

Table 3.2 Consolidated Debt Summary

Each month, David pays the full $1,270 he has earmarked for debt payment towards his single loan. He continues to do this until the debt is paid off.

Consolidation Final Results	
Months to Pay Off	18
Total Interest Paid	$860

Table 3.3 Consolidation Final Result

Scenario B (Snowball)

David feels he will need the psychological boost the Snowball method provides to keep him motivated while paying off his debts. He selects this method and organizes his debts from smallest to largest balance.

Snowball Debt Summary

Debt Name	Amount Owed	Minimum Payment
Macys	$200	$5
MasterCard	$500	$15
Visa	$3,000	$75
Car Loan	$8,000	$250
Student Loan	$10,000	$205
Total	$21,700	$550

Table 3.4 Snowball Debt Summary

Each month, David pays the required minimum on each debt, and then applies all budgeted Wealth-Building funds to the smallest remaining debt(s). He continues to do this, moving progressively towards the larger debts, until all are paid off.

Snowball Month 1 Payment Summary

Debt Name	Amount Owed	Minimum Payment	Wealth-Building Payment	Total Payment
Macys	$200	$5	$195	$200
MasterCard	$500	$15	$485	$500
Visa	$3,000	$75	$40	$115
Car Loan	$8,000	$250	$0	$250
Student Loan	$10,000	$205	$0	$205
Total	$21,700	$550	$720	$1,270

Table 3.5 Snowball Month 1 Payment Summary

After only one month, David has already eliminated two of his smaller debts. He feels his motivation growing and begins to become more enthusiastic about his plan.

Snowball Month 2 Payment Summary

Debt Name	Amount Owed	Minimum Payment	Wealth-Building Payment	Total Payment
Macys	$0	$0	$0	$0
MasterCard	$0	$0	$0	$0
Visa	$2,885	$75	$740	$815
Car Loan	$7,750	$250	$0	$250
Student Loan	$9,795	$205	$0	$205
Total	$20,430	$530	$740	$1,270

Table 3.6 Snowball Month 2 Payment Summary

In the second month, David makes a payment of $815 ($75 + $740) toward a debt, which he had previously only paid the minimum ($75). He can feel the momentum building.

Snowball Month 3 Payment Summary

Debt Name	Amount Owed	Minimum Payment	Wealth-Building Payment	Total Payment
Macys	$0	$0	$0	$0
MasterCard	$0	$0	$0	$0
Visa	$2,070	$75	$740	$815
Car Loan	$7,500	$250	$0	$250
Student Loan	$9,590	$205	$0	$205
Total	$19,160	$530	$740	$1,270

Table 3.7 Snowball Month 3 Payment Summary

David continues to apply the Snowball method for several more months until all his debts are eliminated.

Snowball Final Results	
Months to Pay Off	18
Total Interest Paid	$870

Table 3.8 Snowball Final Results

Scenario C (High Interest First)

David chooses the High Interest First method. He starts by organizing his debts from largest to smallest interest rate.

High Interest First Debt Summary

Debt Name	Amount Owed	Interest Rate
Visa	$3,000	18.0%
MasterCard	$500	17.5%
Macys	$200	15.0%
Car Loan	$8,000	5.0%
Student Loan	$10,000	4.0%
Total	$21,700	

Table 3.9 High Interest First Debt Summary

Each month, David pays the required minimum on each debt, then applies all budgeted Wealth-Building funds ($720) to the remaining debt(s) with the highest interest rate. He continues to do this, moving progressively towards debts with lower interest rates, until all are paid in full.

High Interest First Month 1 Payment Summary

Debt Name	Amount Owed	Interest Rate	Minimum Payment	Wealth-Building Payment	Total Payment
Visa	$3,000	18.0%	$75	$720	$795
MasterCard	$500	17.5%	$15	$0	$15
Macys	$200	15.0%	$5	$0	$5
Car Loan	$8,000	5.0%	$250	$0	$250
Student Loan	$10,000	4.0%	$205	$0	$205
Total	$21,700		$550	$720	$1,270

Table 3.10 High Interest First Month 1 Payment Summary

In the first month, David uses all of the funds allocated to Wealth-Building to pay the debt with the highest interest rate.

High Interest First Month 2 Payment Summary

Debt Name	Amount Owed	Interest Rate	Minimum Payment	Wealth-Building Payment	Total Payment
Visa	$2,205	18.0%	$75	$720	$795
MasterCard	$485	17.5%	$15	$0	$15
Macys	$195	15.0%	$5	$0	$5
Car Loan	$7,750	5.0%	$250	$0	$250
Student Loan	$9,795	4.0%	$205	$0	$205
Total	$20,430		$550	$720	$1,270

Table 3.11 High Interest First Month 2 Payment Summary

In month 2, David again uses his Wealth-Building funds to pay down the debt with the highest interest rate. He continues to do this until that debt is eliminated.

In month 5, after he finishes paying off his highest interest rate debt, David takes the total payment he was applying to it ($795) and adds it to the total payment on the debts which have the next highest interest rates.

High Interest First Month 5 Payment Summary

Debt Name	Amount Owed	Interest Rate	Minimum Payment	Wealth-Building Payment	Total Payment
Visa	$0	18.0%	$0	$0	$0
MasterCard	$260	17.5%	$15	$245	$260
Macys	$180	15.0%	$5	$175	$180
Car Loan	$7,000	5.0%	$250	$375	$625
Student Loan	$9,180	4.0%	$205	$0	$205
Total	$16,620		$475	$795	$1,270

Table 3.12 High Interest First Month 5 Payment Summary

David continues to apply the High Interest First method for several more months until all his debts are eliminated.

High Interest First Final Results	
Months to Pay Off	18
Total Interest Paid	$865

Table 3.13 High Interest First Final Results

> **Note:** If David were to continue paying only the minimum required for each of his debts instead of implementing one of the strategies described, it would take him 62 months and cost over $3,400 in interest to become debt free.

Following the completion of Phase 3, David's updated budget is as follows.

David's Phase 3 Budget

Fixed Expenses		Wealth-Building		Flexible Expenses	
Rent	$600	Saving, Investing, and Paying Debt	$1,270	Eating Out	$200
Utilities	$75			Entertainment	$150
Car Insurance	$75			Hobbies	$100
Groceries	$100			Gym	$50
Gasoline	$50			Cable TV	$0
Health Insurance	$150			Internet	$75
Minimum Debt Payments	$0			Mobile Phone	$120
				Subscriptions	$50
				Shopping	$55
Total	$1,050	Total	$1,270	Total	$800
% of Income	33.7%	% of Income	40.7%	% of Income	25.6%

Total	$3,120
% of Income	100%

Current Savings	$1,440

Table 3.14 David's Phase 3 Budget

PHASE 4

Emergency Fund

Congratulations! Give yourself a pat on the back. If you've made it this far, you're either debt-free or well on your way to becoming so. This is a huge accomplishment, but it's not time to rest yet. By eliminating most of your debt, you may have freed up a significant amount of money in your monthly budget. The money that was previously being used to pay creditors is now totally unallocated. With this extra money in hand, you could allow yourself to fall back into old, bad spending habits. Or you can remain disciplined and continue to speed towards Financial Freedom. If you stop here you might quickly find yourself back in the financial situation you started with. So don't give up; we're just getting to the good parts!

As mentioned at the beginning of *Phase 2: The First $1,000*, your objective in Phase 4 will be to complete your emergency fund by saving enough money to cover 6-12 months of living expenses. Take out your trusty budget and let's begin!

Step 1

You're done paying debt! Update your budget to reflect this. Move all the money in the Fixed Expenses category, which is allocated to paying debt minimums, to the Wealth-Building category. Next, add up all of your fixed and flexible expenses to get your new and improved monthly expense total.

Step 2

After budgeting and paying off debt, you should have at least 20% of your income available to finish building your emergency fund. Let's start building. Multiply the monthly expense total you calculated in Step 1 by 12. This gives you the amount of money you would need to cover one year of fixed and flexible expenses. This is your new savings goal.

> **Note:** Although we highly recommend you save enough money in your emergency fund to cover an entire year of expenses, some may feel this is more than they need. A larger emergency fund will provide a more durable safety net, but as long as you have saved enough money to cover at least 6 months of expenses, we consider that an acceptable amount. If you choose to save a lesser amount for your emergency fund, be sure to adjust the numbers in your calculations (e.g. Use 8 instead of 12 if you are saving for eight months of expenses).

Step 3

Update your direct deposit or automatic transfer settings so that each month the new higher amount allocated to your Wealth-Building category is automatically deposited into the emergency fund account you created in *Phase 2: The First $1,000* (This account will soon grow well beyond $1,000!). As previously noted, it is very important this happens automatically so there is less opportunity to "unintentionally", spend the money.

Step 4

Review Step 2 of *Phase 2: The First $1,000*, for ways to reduce spending and increase income. Implement any of the strategies that inspire you.

Step 5

Continue to maintain your budget and watch as your emergency fund grows!

CASE STUDY 4

After completing Phase 3, David updated his budget by taking all of the funds that were previously assigned to minimum debt payments and adding them to his Wealth-Building total.

David's Updated Budget

Fixed Expenses		Wealth-Building		Flexible Expenses	
Rent	$600	Saving, Investing, and Paying Debt	$1,270	Eating Out	$200
Utilities	$75			Entertainment	$150
Car Insurance	$75			Hobbies	$100
Groceries	$100			Gym	$50
Gasoline	$50			Cable TV	$0
Health Insurance	$150			Internet	$75
Minimum Debt Payments	$0			Mobile Phone	$120
				Subscriptions	$50
				Shopping	$55
Total	$1,050	Total	$1,270	Total	$800
% of Income	33.7%	% of Income	40.7%	% of Income	25.6%

Total	$3,120
% of Income	100.0%

Current Savings	$1,440

Table 4.1 David's Updated Budget

David adds his fixed and flexible expense totals together to get his monthly expense total. He then multiplies this number by 12 to determine how much he will need to cover one full year of expenses.

$$Total\ Monthly\ Expenses = \$1,050 + \$800 = \mathbf{\$1,850}$$

$$1\ Year\ of\ Expenses = \$1,850 * 12 = \mathbf{\$22,200}$$

At work, David sets up direct deposit so that the budgeted amount ($1,270) is automatically sent to his savings account each month. After just 17 months, David has amassed an emergency fund large enough to cover all his expenses for a full year.

Monthly Savings Record	
David's Initial Savings	$1,440
Savings After 1 Month	$2,710
Savings After 2 Months	$3,980
Savings After 3 Months	$5,250
Savings After 4 Months	$6,520
Savings After 5 Months	$7,790
Savings After 6 Months	$9,060
Savings After 7 Months	$10,330
Savings After 8 Months	$11,600
Savings After 9 Months	$12,870
Savings After 10 Months	$14,140
Savings After 11 Months	$15,410
Savings After 12 Months	$16,680

Savings After 13 Months	$17,950
Savings After 14 Months	$19,220
Savings After 15 Months	$20,490
Savings After 16 Months	$21,760
Savings After 17 Months	**$23,030**

Table 4.2 Monthly Savings Record

David updates his budget with his new savings total.

David's Phase 4 Budget

Fixed Expenses		Flexible Expenses		Wealth-Building	
Rent	$600	Saving, Investing, and Paying Debt	$1,270	Eating Out	$200
Utilities	$75			Entertainment	$150
Car Insurance	$75			Hobbies	$100
Groceries	$100			Gym	$50
Gasoline	$50			Cable TV	$0
Health Insurance	$150			Internet	$75
Minimum Debt Payments	$0			Mobile Phone	$120
				Subscriptions	$50
				Shopping	$55
Total	$1,050	Total	$1,270	Total	$800
% of Income	33.7%	% of Income	40.7%	% of Income	25.6%

Total	$3,120
% of Income	100.0%

Current Savings	$23,030

Table 4.3 David's Phase 4 Budget

PHASE 5

401(k)s and Roth IRAs

You've meticulously laid out your budget so you know where every dollar is going. You're totally debt-free (or at least free of all non-mortgage debt). You've got a large enough emergency fund saved to weather any storm that life throws at you. Your finances are in a stable place. This is a wonderful accomplishment! Now that financial stability has been reached, the next step is to begin multiplying your money.

The best way to grow your money over time is by investing it. We believe the best investment vehicles currently available to us normal folks are **tax-advantaged** retirement accounts, specifically **401(k)** and **Roth Individual Retirement Account (IRA)** plans. If your employer offers a 401(k) plan (or **403(b)**, or **457**, etc.), enrolling is a top priority. This is especially true if your employer provides any amount of dollar matching. Dollar matching gives you free money, something you should never pass up. If you've already hit your 401(k) yearly contribution limit ($18,500 per 2018 Internal Revenue Service regulations), or don't have a comparable retirement plan offered at your place of work, your next best option will be to contribute to a Roth IRA. Both of these accounts will provide you with solid growth and give you tax benefits that non-retirement accounts don't offer.

In *Phase 4: Emergency Fund*, money previously allocated to paying debt was shifted to the Wealth-Building category in your budget. Since the original budget allocated 20% of your income to Wealth-Building, it is possible you now have well over 20% going towards this category. We realize you may have made some significant sacrifices in order to reach this position. If you've come to a point where flexible spending is significantly less than 30% of your income or fixed spending is significantly less than 50% of your income, now is the time to decide whether you want to continue to live this way or if you'd like to shift some money back to these categories. Now that you are successfully living on your budget and debt-free, with 6-12 months of living expenses saved, you've earned the right to enjoy some luxuries, if you so choose. As long as you stay within the boundaries of the 50/20/30 budget guidelines, you are free to re-allocate your budget as you see fit. Keep in mind, however, the money you save from this point on will begin to grow exponentially. Every extra dollar saved will have a huge impact on the speed at which you attain true Financial Freedom.

Step 1

Calculate your current budget allocation percentage for the Wealth-Building category. Do this by taking the dollar amount you currently have allocated to the Wealth-Building category and dividing it by your total monthly after-tax income.

$$\textit{Wealth Building Percentage} = \textit{wealth building} \div \textit{after tax income}$$

Step 2

Enroll in your employer-sponsored 401(k) plan (if your company does not offer a 401(k) or comparable plan, move on to Step 3). Investigate whether your company matches your contributions and, if so, how much they will match. Contribute enough to get the maximum possible dollar match. If this requires you to contribute the full amount you currently have allocated to Wealth-Building, then contribute that amount and move on to *Phase 6: Investing*. If you still have remaining funds allocated to Wealth-Building after maximizing your employer's dollar matching, continue to Step 3.

Step 3

If your employer doesn't offer a 401k or comparable retirement plan option or you've already contributed enough to maximize your plan's dollar matching, the next step is to open a Roth IRA with an online investment broker (see *Additional Information* for a list of recommended brokers). Once you've opened the account, you must be aware of two things before beginning your contributions. First, individuals and married couples that earn over a certain income are not eligible to contribute directly to a Roth IRA. Review the current Internal Revenue Service rules on this topic at www.irs.com before making any contributions. Second, Roth IRA's have a yearly contribution limit ($5,500 for someone under 50 per 2018 Internal Revenue Service regulations). Be sure not to go over this limit when contributing. Once you've established that you are eligible to contribute, set up automatic withdrawals from your checking account to be deposited directly into your Roth IRA each month. Contribute as much as your remaining Wealth-Building budget allows, without going over the yearly contribution limit.

> **Note:** If your earnings are above the income limit for eligibility to contribute directly to a Roth IRA, you can still legally contribute via the **backdoor Roth IRA contribution method**. Review the description of this method in the *Additional Information* section and conduct further research on your own to decide if this is the right approach for you.

Step 4

At this point, if you've contributed enough to achieve the maximum company match in your 401(k) and/or you've maxed out your Roth IRA yearly contribution, you're in excellent shape. Anything remaining in the Wealth-Building category of your budget should be put towards reaching the maximum yearly 401(k) contribution limit. If you reach this contribution limit as well and still have additional funds available, you'll learn what to do with the remainder in *Phase 6: Investing*.

Note: We will discuss exactly how to invest your money in *Phase 6: Investing* (e.g. Stocks, Bonds, Options, Index funds, Mutual funds etc.).

CASE STUDY 5

David has well over 20% of his income allocated to Wealth-Building. As a result, he now has the ability to increase his expenditures a bit and still meet the guidelines of a 50/20/30 budget. He decides he'd like to renew his cable TV service. He does so and updates his budget accordingly.

David's Updated Budget

Fixed Expenses		Wealth-Building		Flexible Expenses	
Rent	$600	Saving, Investing, and Paying Debt	$1,120	Eating Out	$200
Utilities	$75			Entertainment	$150
Car Insurance	$75			Hobbies	$100
Groceries	$100			Gym	$50
Gasoline	$50			Cable TV (Cable renewed)	$150
Health Insurance	$150			Internet	$75
Minimum Debt Payments	$0			Mobile Phone	$120
				Subscriptions	$50
				Shopping	$55
Total	$1,050	Total	$1,120	Total	$950
% of Income	33.7%	% of Income	35.9%	% of Income	30.4%

Total	$3,120
% of Income	100.0%

Current Savings	$23,030

Table 5.1 David's Updated Budget

At work, David speaks with his manager to requests information about the company's 401(k) plan. Upon reviewing the information, he learns that his employer will match 50% of any contribution he makes, up to 10% of his salary. This means, for every dollar David contributes, up to 10% of his salary, his employer will give him 50 cents for free.

David's current monthly income is $3,120. In order to receive the full employer match each month, David must contribute $312 (i.e. 10% of his income) to his 401(k). His employer will contribute an additional 50% of that amount, or $156, via their contribution matching program.

David calculates his current Wealth-Building percentage.

$$Wealth\ Building\ Percentage = \$1{,}120 \div \$3{,}120 = \mathbf{35.9}\%$$

The percentage of David's income allocated to Wealth-Building is greater than the 10% required, therefore, he will be able to contribute enough to earn the maximum employer match.

> **Note**: For simplification purposes, taxes are ignored in the example above. In reality, 401(k) contributions are made from pre-tax income. Every dollar contributed to a 401(k) investment account lowers an individual's taxable income. This tax-advantaged status is one of the reasons we recommend maximizing retirement account investing before pursuing other investment opportunities.

Next, David determines the amount he can contribute to a Roth IRA. After his initial 401(k) contribution, he has $808 (i.e. $1,120 - $312) remaining in his Wealth-Building funds. On www.irs.com, David finds that the IRS allows a maximum Roth IRA contribution of $5,500 per year. Spread over 12 months, this equates to a $458 contribution per month (i.e. $5,500 / 12 months). With $808 per month in Wealth-Building funds still available, David will be able to make the maximum contribution to his Roth IRA.

David has now budgeted enough to achieve the maximum company match in his 401(k) and to fully fund his Roth IRA. He uses the remaining $350 (i.e. $808 - $458) of his Wealth-Building funds to increase his 401(k) contribution.

David updates his budget to reflect the 401(k) and Roth IRA contributions he will make.

David's Phase 5 Budget

Fixed Expenses		Wealth-Building		Flexible Expenses	
Rent	$600	401(k) for company match (10%)	$312	Eating Out	$200
Utilities	$75	Roth IRA	$458	Entertainment	$150
Car Insurance	$75	401(k) Additional contribution	$350	Hobbies	$100
Groceries	$100			Gym	$50
Gasoline	$50			Cable TV	$150
Health Insurance	$150			Internet	$75
Minimum Debt Payments	$0			Mobile Phone	$120
				Subscriptions	$50
				Shopping	$55
Total	$1,050	Total	$1,120	Total	$950
% of Income	33.7%	% of Income	35.9%	% of Income	30.4%

Total	$3,120
% of Income	100.0%

Current Savings	$23,030

Table 5.2 David's Phase 5 Budget

PHASE 6

Investing

There are an almost infinite number of ways to invest money. If you have limited knowledge or experience in this area, however, it can be a very intimidating process. In Phase 6 we will walk you, step-by-step, through a simple and easy-to-follow investment strategy, which takes advantage of the continuous growth of the stock market over time. Hopefully, this strategy will ease any fears you may have.

Step 1

Subtract your current age from 120. The resulting number is the percentage of your investment amount that you will use to purchase **stocks**. The remainder will be invested in **bonds**. This distribution will allow your money to grow with the volatility of the stock market, while still providing stability, via the bond market, for those who are investing later in life.

$$Stock\ Investment\ Percentage = 120 - current\ age$$

$$Bond\ Investment\ Percentage = 100\% - stock\ investment\ percentage$$

Step 2

Multiply your total investment amount (i.e. Wealth-Building funds) by your stock investment percentage to calculate the dollar amount you will use to buy stocks. Subtract this amount from the total investment amount, to derive how much you will use to buy bonds.

Stock Investment Amount

$$= total\ investment\ amount * stock\ investment\ percentage$$

Bond Investment Amount

$$= total\ investment\ amount - stock\ investment\ amount$$

Step 3

Review the amount currently allocated to Wealth-Building in your monthly budget. Multiply this number by 12 to determine your yearly Wealth-Building total.

If the amount currently allocated to Wealth-Building per year is less than the maximum total contribution allowed per year towards the retirement account(s) you hold ($5,500 per year for Roth IRAs and $18,500 per year for 401(k), as of 2018), you will do all of your investing in this/these retirement account(s). You should always leverage the tax-advantaged status of available retirement accounts before doing any investing in a taxable account (see *Phase 5: 401(k)s and Roth IRAs)*. This will help you achieve the maximum benefit. If your yearly Wealth-Building allocation meets this criterion, you will skip Step 4 and, instead, move on to Step 5.

Conversely, if you find that your yearly Wealth-Building allocation is greater than the amount needed to max-out your retirement account(s), proceed to Step 4 to begin non-retirement account investing.

Step 4

Open a new taxable investment account, if possible, with the same broker you are using for your Roth IRA (see *Phase 5: 401(k)s and Roth IRAs*). Just as you did with your Roth IRA, set up regular automatic withdrawals from your checking account, to be deposited into your new investment account. The total amount deposited per month should be equal to the remainder of your budget's monthly Wealth-Building allocation, after contributing the maximum to your retirement account(s) (i.e. 401(k) and/or Roth IRA).

Step 5

In your investment account(s), use all the funds designated for stock purchases (see Steps 1 and 2) to buy a total stock market, or **Standard & Poor's 500 (S&P 500), exchange traded fund (ETF)**. Next, use all the money designated for bond purchases to buy a total bond market ETF. Vanguard Total Stock Market ETF (VTI) and Vanguard S&P 500 ETF (VOO) are examples of total stock market and S&P 500 ETFs, respectively, and Vanguard Total Bond

Market ETF (BND) is an example of a total bond market ETF. You are free to invest in these examples or to select your own comparable ETFs (see *Additional Information* for further recommendations). If you do select your own, be sure the **expense ratio** (the fee associated with owning the ETF) is <u>less than</u> 0.2%. You can find the expense ratio for a particular ETF, as well as other EFT options, by doing a quick search online.

So, what is the basis of this investment strategy? Why commit such a large percentage of your **investment portfolio** to stocks? The answer is, historical performance. Over the last 100+ years, the stock market has grown at an average rate of 7-10% annually. To some, this may not sound like a significant growth rate. However, when it is paired with **compounding interest**, money invested in the stock market will increase in value exponentially over time. It should be noted, the stock market does not always grow at a consistent rate. There have been years when the market has suffered huge losses and years when there have been huge gains. But, over the long run, there has been steady growth. In order to take advantage of this growth, our strategy places a large portion of invested funds into ETFs that track the overall stock market. We specifically selected ETFs as opposed to **index funds** for multiple reasons, one of which is their extremely low expense ratios. VTI for instance, has an expense ratio of only 0.05%, which amounts to just 50 cents for every $1,000 invested. In addition to this advantage, ETFs do not require a minimum initial investment and give investors the flexibility to buy and sell at any time during market hours. When paired together, all of these benefits give ETFs a slight edge over index funds, for someone who is new to investing.

Note: As the size of your portfolio grows and you become more comfortable as an investor, you may decide that index funds are more advantageous for your situation. It would be perfectly fine to begin investing in index funds at that point, as long as the funds you select are comparable to the EFTs we have described, in both makeup (i.e. total stock market funds or S&P 500 funds and total bond market funds) and pricing (i.e. expense ratio less than 0.2%).

We believe that investing in **broad-based** stock funds is the best way to produce consistent, long-term financial gains, and history seems to agree. So why add bonds into the equation? Bonds are much less volatile than stocks. As a result, they serve as a stabilizing force in an investment portfolio. Typically, the gains you earn from investing in bonds will be smaller than those produced by stocks, but the losses will be smaller as well. As we age, we have less time to allow our investment portfolio to recover when it suffers a large loss. The formula in Step 1 is in place to address this issue. It determines what percentage of funds should be directed towards each type of investment, giving an older individual a larger allotment of bonds, while a younger person will have primarily stocks in their portfolio.

Note: Most retirement accounts will not allow you to purchase ETFs. Look instead for an index fund that tracks the overall stock market or S&P 500 and one that tracks the overall bond market. Substitute these funds for the recommended ETFs.

Step 6

When a company makes money, its **board of directors** may decide to distribute some of those earnings to the company's owners. The portion of the earnings that the owners receive is called a **dividend**. After implementing your investment strategy you will begin to accumulate stock. This means you will be part owner of many different companies and, as a result, it is very likely you will receive dividends. All dividends you receive should be reinvested via enrollment in your broker's **dividend reinvestment program (DRIP)**.

When you enroll in a DRIP, any dividends you receive will be automatically reinvested for you. Sign-in to your investment account online and enroll manually by accessing your account settings. If you are unable to determine how to enroll, contact your broker directly and ask them to configure your account so that all dividends are automatically reinvested. It is extremely important that you do this. Reinvesting dividends cuts down on transaction costs, gives you the ability to purchase **fractional shares**, and automatically puts your dividend income to use. Dividend reinvestment is one of the most impactful measures you can take to help your investments grow.

Step 7

Continue to automatically deposit money into your account(s) every month (or pay period) and continue to purchase stocks and bonds at the recommended percentages. Watch as your money grows exponentially over time.

> **Note:** Though there are some brokers with zero transaction fees (e.g. Robinhood.com), most brokers will charge you a few dollars every time you buy or sell **securities** (i.e. stocks or bonds). In order to avoid excessive fees, we advise that you make such transactions no more than 1-2 times per month. This is one area where index funds have an advantage over ETFs, as index funds typically do not charge transactions fees.

Alternate Investment Strategy

Self-managed investing, as described above, is our recommended course of action, however, if you still do not feel confident enough to personally implement the investment strategy we've outlined, there is an alternative.

We do not recommend traditional personal financial advisors, as they tend to have high fees and produce mediocre results. However, there is a class of investment advising companies that we do endorse, **robo-advisors**. These companies provide automated financial portfolio management with very little human interference. They tend to provide solid returns at a relatively low cost. Robo-advisors typically charge a small fee for their services, so investing through one will most likely be more expensive than doing it on your own. However, you will enjoy the added advantage of having a professional investment company in your corner, helping you make decisions. In addition, many robo-advisors offer benefits such as automatic **account rebalancing, tax-loss harvesting** (for non-retirement, taxable accounts), and custom portfolio **diversification**. If you are leaning toward utilizing this investment approach, you will find that there are many great robo-advisor's currently available. Do your own research and decide which advisor is best for you. Wealthfront.com and Betterment.com are our current top two recommendations for someone beginning to invest using a robo-advisor. These two companies have led the way in the robo-investing industry and are two of the largest and most established options available (see *Additional Information* for more options).

CASE STUDY 6

David has just turned 39 years old. He calculates his stock investment percentage and bond investment percentage as follows.

$$Stock\ Investment\ Percentage = 120 - 39 = \mathbf{81}\%$$

$$Bond\ Investment\ Percentage = 100\% - 81\% = \mathbf{19}\%$$

Based on these calculations, David plans to use 81% of his Wealth-Building funds to invest in stocks and 19% to invest in bonds.

David consults his budget to determine the contribution amount he has assigned to his retirement accounts. Using these quantities, and the investment percentages he just calculated, David works out the dollar amount of each investment.

David's Current Budget

Fixed Expenses		Wealth-Building		Flexible Expenses	
Rent	$600	401(k)	$662	Eating Out	$200
Utilities	$75	Roth IRA	$458	Entertainment	$150
Car Insurance	$75			Hobbies	$100
Groceries	$100			Gym	$50
Gasoline	$50			Cable TV	$150
Health Insurance	$150			Internet	$75
Minimum Debt Payments	$0			Mobile Phone	$120
				Subscriptions	$50
				Shopping	$55
Total	$1,050	Total	$1,120	Total	$950
% of Income	33.7%	% of Income	35.9%	% of Income	30.4%

Total	$3,120
% of Income	100.0%

Current Savings	$23,030

Table 6.1 David's Current Budget

401(k)

$$401(k) \; Stock \; Investment \; Amount = \$662 * 81\% = \mathbf{\$536}$$

$$401(k) \; Bond \; Investment \; Amount = \$662 - \$536 = \mathbf{\$126}$$

Roth IRA

$$Roth \; IRA \; Stock \; Investment \; Amount = \$458 * 81\% = \mathbf{\$371}$$

$$Roth \; IRA \; Bond \; Investment \; Amount = \$458 - \$371 = \mathbf{\$87}$$

Based on 2018 IRS guidelines, it would take a total of $24,000 (i.e. $18,500 for 401(k) + $5,500 for Roth IRA) to contribute the maximum allowed per year to both a Roth IRA and 401(k). David multiplies his current Wealth-Building allocation by 12 to determine if his yearly Wealth-Building total would be enough.

$$Yearly\ Wealth\ Building\ Total = \$1,120 * 12 = \$13,440$$

Since David's yearly Wealth-Building total is less than the $24,000 limit, he will be able to do all of his investing in his tax-advantaged retirement accounts and does not need to open any additional investment accounts.

At work, David sets up his 401(k) account so that $662 is automatically deposited each month. He then looks through the available funds and assigns 81% ($536) of all contributions to be invested in an S&P 500 index fund and 19% ($126) to be invested in a US bond index fund.

Outside of work, David opens a Roth IRA account with an online investment broker. He sets up automatic deposits for this account so that, each month, $458 is pulled from his checking account. David then contacts his broker and enrolls in their dividend reinvestment program. Once every month, David logs into his Roth IRA account and purchases $371 (81%) worth of total stock market ETFs and $87 (19%) worth of total bond market ETFs.

David's Final Budget

Fixed Expenses		Wealth-Building		Flexible Expenses	
Rent	$600	401(k) Stocks	$536	Eating Out	$200
Utilities	$75	401(k) Bonds	$126	Entertainment	$150
Car Insurance	$75	Roth IRA Stocks	$371	Hobbies	$100
Groceries	$100	Roth IRA Bonds	$87	Gym	$50
Gasoline	$50			Cable TV	$150
Health Insurance	$150			Internet	$75
Minimum Debt Payments	$0			Mobile Phone	$120
				Subscriptions	$50
				Shopping	$55
Total	$1,050	Total	$1,120	Total	$950
% of Income	33.7%	% of Income	35.9%	% of Income	30.4%

Total	$3,120
% of Income	100.0%

Current Savings	$23,030

Table 6.2 David's Final Budget

What's next?

Budget implemented? Check. Debt eliminated? Check. Emergency fund established? Check. Investments working for you? Check. Congratulations! You've made it. You have worked your butt off and transformed your life. By continuing to utilize the lessons learned in this book, you will be able to enjoy life without the stress of worrying about money. In time, you'll be able to retire in a financially secure position, with a significant nest egg available to maintain your lifestyle. You are on the fast track to Financial Freedom. Keep moving forward and you will undoubtedly reach it, if you haven't already.

Our final recommendation is that you take what you have learned in this book and share it with your friends, family members, and anyone else who is willing to listen. The more people we empower with the knowledge to become financially free, the better the world will become!

Visit www.The6PhasesOfBuildingWealth.com for additional information.

Additional Information

Recommendations

Investment Brokers

Robinhood (Robinhood.com)

Ally Invest (Ally.com)

OptionsXpress (OptionsXpress.com)

The Vanguard Group (Vanguard.com)

Charles Schwab (Schwab.com)

E*Trade Financial (US.Etrade.com)

TD Ameritrade (TDAmeritrade.com)

Budgeting Tools

Spreadsheet (Google Docs, Microsoft Excel, Apple Numbers)

Mint (Mint.com)

Power Wallet (PowerWallet.com)

Personal Capital (PersonalCapital.com)

Robo-Advisors

Wealthfront (Wealthfront.com)

Betterment (Betterment.com)

Charles Schwab Intelligent Portfolios (Intelligent.Schwab.com)

Wisebanyan (Wisebanyan.com)

High-Yield Savings Accounts

Ally Bank (Ally.com)

Synchrony Bank (Synchronybank.com)

Barclays (Banking.BarclaysUS.com)

CIT Bank (BankOnCIT.com)

Goldman Sachs Bank (GSBank.com)

Total Stock Market and S&P 500 ETFs

Vanguard Total Stock Market ETF (VTI)

Vanguard 500 Index Fund (VOO)

Schwab US Broad Market ETF (SCHB)

SPDR S&P 500 ETF Trust (SPY)

iShares S&P 1500 Index Fund (ITOT)

Total Stock Market and S&P 500 Index Funds

Vanguard Total Stock Market Index Fund Admiral Shares (VTSAX)

Vanguard Total Stock Market Index Fund Investor Shares (VTSMX)

Schwab Total Stock Market Index Fund (SWTSX)

Total Bond Market ETFs

Vanguard Total Bond Market ETF (BND)

iShare Core U.S. Aggregate Bond Fund (AGG)

Schwab US Aggregate Bond Fund (SCHZ)

iShares Core Total USD Bond Market ETF (IUSB)

Total Bond Market Index Funds

Vanguard Total Bond Market Index Fund Admiral Shares (VBTLX)

Vanguard Total Bond Market Index Fund Investor Shares (VBMFX)

Glossary

401(k) Plan - A 401(k) plan is a qualified employer-established plan to which eligible employees may make salary deferral (salary reduction) contributions on a post-tax and/or pretax basis. Employers offering a 401(k) plan may make matching or non-elective contributions to the plan on behalf of eligible employees and may also add a profit-sharing feature to the plan. Earnings in a 401(k) plan accrue on a tax-deferred basis. (Investopedia.com, 2017)

403(b) Plan - A 403(b) plan is a retirement plan for specific employees of public schools, tax-exempt organizations and certain ministers. These plans can invest in either annuities or mutual funds. A 403(b) plan is another name for a tax-sheltered annuity plan. The features of a 403(b) plan are comparable to those found in a 401(k) plan. (Investopedia.com, 2017)

457 Plan - A 457 is a nonqualified, employer-sponsored deferred compensation plan for employees of state and local government agencies and some tax-exempt organizations. Eligible employees are allowed to make salary deferral contributions to the 457 plan. Earnings grow on a tax-deferred basis and contributions are not taxed until the assets are distributed from the plan. (Investopedia.com, 2017)

Account Rebalancing - Rebalancing is the process of realigning the weightings of a portfolio's of assets. Rebalancing involves periodically buying or selling assets in a portfolio to maintain an original desired level of asset allocation. (Investopedia.com, 2017)

After-Tax Income - After-tax income is the amount of money that an individual or company has left over after all federal, state and withholding taxes have been deducted from taxable income. (Investopedia.com, 2017)

Annual Percentage Rate (APR) - An annual percentage rate (APR) is the annual rate charged for borrowing or earned through an investment, and is expressed as a percentage that represents the actual yearly cost of funds over the term of a loan. This includes any fees or additional costs associated with the transaction but does not take compounding into account. (Investopedia.com, 2017)

Backdoor Roth IRA Contribution Method - A method that taxpayers can use to place retirement savings in a Roth IRA, even if their income is higher than the maximum the IRS allows for regular Roth IRA contributions. "Backdoor Roth IRA" is an informal name for a complicated, but IRS-sanctioned, method that lets high-income taxpayers take a roundabout path to putting money in a Roth; it is not the formal name for an official type of retirement account.

The backdoor Roth is an option for higher-income taxpayers because, since 2010, the IRS hasn't had income limits that restrict who can convert a traditional IRA to Roth IRA. As a result, taxpayers who ordinarily couldn't contribute to a Roth can instead make a non-tax-deductible contribution to a traditional IRA and then convert the traditional IRA to a Roth IRA. (Investopedia.com, 2017)

Board of Directors - A board of directors (B of D) is a group of individuals that are elected as, or elected to act as, representatives of the stockholders to establish corporate management related policies and to make decisions on major company issues. Every public company must have a board of directors. Some private and nonprofit companies have a board of directors as well. (Investopedia.com, 2017)

Bond - A bond is a debt investment in which an investor loans money to an entity (typically corporate or governmental), which borrows the funds for a defined period of time at a variable or fixed interest rate. Bonds are used by companies, municipalities, states and sovereign governments to raise money and finance a variety of projects and activities. Owners of bonds are debt holders, or creditors, of the issuer. (Investopedia.com, 2017)

Broad-Based (Broad-Based Index) - An index designed to reflect the movement of the entire market. (Investopedia.com, 2017)

Brick-and-Mortar - Brick and mortar is a traditional street-side business that deals with its customers face-to-face in an office or store that the business owns or rents. The local grocery store and the corner bank are examples of brick-and-mortar companies. Brick-and-mortar businesses can find it difficult to compete with web-based businesses like Amazon.com, Inc. because the latter usually have lower operating costs and greater flexibility. (Investopedia.com, 2017)

Compound Interest - Compound interest (or compounding interest) is interest calculated on the initial principal and also on the accumulated interest of previous periods of a deposit or loan. Thought to have originated in 17th-century Italy, compound interest can be thought of as "interest on interest," and will make a sum grow at a faster rate than simple interest, which is calculated only on the principal amount. (Investopedia.com, 2017)

Diversification - Diversification is a risk management technique that mixes a wide variety of investments within a portfolio. The rationale behind this technique contends that a portfolio constructed of different kinds of investments will, on average, yield higher returns and pose a lower risk than any individual investment found within the portfolio. (Investopedia.com, 2017)

Dividend - A dividend is a distribution of a portion of a company's earnings, decided by the board of directors, to a class of its shareholders. Dividends can be issued as cash payments, as shares of stock, or other property. (Investopedia.com, 2017)

Dividend Reinvestment Program (DRIP) - A dividend reinvestment plan (DRIP) is offered by a corporation that allows investors to reinvest their cash dividends by purchasing additional shares or fractional shares on the dividend payment date. A DRIP is an excellent way to increase the value of an investment. Most DRIPs allow investors to buy shares commission-free and at a significant discount to the current share price, and do not allow reinvestments much lower than $10. This term is sometimes abbreviated as "DRP." (Investopedia.com, 2017)

Exchange Traded Fund (ETF) - An ETF, or exchange-traded fund, is a marketable security that tracks an index, a commodity, bonds, or a basket of assets like an index fund. Unlike mutual funds, an ETF trades like a common stock on a stock exchange. ETFs experience price changes throughout the day as they are bought and sold. ETFs typically have higher daily liquidity and lower fees than mutual fund shares, making them an attractive alternative for individual investors. (Investopedia.com, 2017)

Financial Freedom - Living life with the knowledge that you are totally financially secure and will continue to be so for the remainder of your days.

Fractional Shares - A fractional share is a share of equity that is less than one full share. Fractional shares usually come about from stock splits, dividend reinvestment plans (DRIPs) and similar corporate actions. Normally, fractional shares cannot be acquired from the market, and while they have value to the investor, they can be difficult to sell. (Investopedia.com, 2017)

High-Yield Savings Account - High-yield savings accounts are deposit accounts available through a online or brick-and-mortar banks that pay a higher interest rate (or an annual percentage yield (APY)) than a traditional deposit savings account. (Investopedia.com, 2017)

Index Fund - An index fund is a type of mutual fund with a portfolio constructed to match or track the components of a market index, such as the Standard & Poor's 500 Index (S&P 500). An index mutual fund is said to provide broad market exposure, low operating expenses and low portfolio turnover. These funds adhere to specific rules or standards (e.g. efficient tax management or reducing tracking errors) that stay in place no matter the state of the markets. (Investopedia.com, 2017)

Investment Portfolio - A portfolio is a grouping of financial assets such as stocks, bonds and cash equivalents, as well as their funds counterparts, including mutual, exchange-traded and closed funds. Portfolios are held directly by investors and/or managed by financial professionals. (Investopedia.com, 2017)

Origination Fees - An origination fee is an upfront fee charged by a lender for processing a new loan application, used as compensation for putting the loan in place. (Investopedia.com, 2017)

Revolving Line of Credit - Revolving credit is very similar to a credit card. The lending institution grants you a maximum credit limit, which you can use to make purchases at any time and (usually) on any goods. Many small business owners and corporations use revolving credit to finance capital expansion or as a safeguard in the event of cash flow problems. (Investopedia.com, 2017)

Robo-Advisors - Robo-advisors (robo-advisers) are digital platforms that provide automated, algorithm-driven financial planning services with little to no human supervision. A typical robo-advisor collects information from clients about their financial situation and future goals through an online survey, and then uses the data to offer advice and/or automatically invest client assets. (Investopedia.com, 2017)

Roth Individual Retirement Account (IRA) - Named for Delaware Senator William Roth and established by the Taxpayer Relief Act of 1997, a Roth IRA is an individual retirement plan (a type of qualified retirement plan) that bears many similarities to the traditional IRA. The biggest distinction between the two is how they're taxed. Since traditional IRAs contributions are made with pretax dollars, you pay income tax when you withdraw the money from the account during retirement. Conversely, Roth IRAs are funded with after-tax dollars; the contributions are not tax deductible (although you may be able to take a tax credit of 10 to 50% of the contribution), depending on your income and life situation). But when you start withdrawing funds, these qualified distributions are tax-free. (Investopedia.com, 2017)

Standard & Poor's 500 (S&P 500) – an index of 500 stocks seen as a leading indicator of U.S. equities and a reflection of the performance of the large cap universe, made up of companies selected by economists. The S&P 500 is a market value weighted index and one of the common benchmarks for the U.S. stock market. (Investopedia.com, 2017)

Security - A security is a fungible, negotiable financial instrument that holds some type of monetary value. It represents an ownership position in a publicly-traded corporation (via stock), a creditor relationship with a governmental body or a corporation (represented by owning that entity's bond), or rights to ownership as represented by an option. (Investopedia.com, 2017)

Stock - A stock is a type of security that signifies ownership in a corporation and represents a claim on part of the corporation's assets and earnings. (Investopedia.com, 2017)

Tax-Loss Harvesting - Tax gain/loss harvesting is a strategy of selling securities at a loss to offset a capital gains tax liability. It is typically used to limit the recognition of short-term capital gains, which are normally taxed at higher federal income tax rates than long-term capital gains, though it is also used for long-term capital gains. (Investopedia.com, 2017)

Traditional Individual Retirement Account (IRA) - A traditional individual retirement account (IRA) allows individuals to direct pretax income towards investments that can grow tax-deferred; no capital gains or dividend income is taxed until it is withdrawn. Individual taxpayers are allowed to contribute 100% of any earned compensation up to a specified maximum dollar amount. Contributions to a traditional IRA may be tax-deductible depending on the taxpayer's income, tax-filing status and other factors. (Investopedia.com, 2017)

Unsecured Debt - Unsecured debt is a loan that is not backed by an underlying asset. Unsecured debt includes credit card debt, medical bills, utility bills and other types of loans or credit that were extended without a collateral requirement. This type of debt presents a high risk for lenders, also referred to as the creditor, since they may have to sue for repayment if the borrower doesn't repay the full amount owed. (Investopedia.com, 2017)

Appendix

Equations

1 *Year of Expenses* $= total\ monthly\ expenses * 12$

Wealth Building Percentage $= wealth\ building \div after\ tax\ income$

Stock Investment Percentage $= 120 - current\ age$

Bond Investment Percentage $= 100\% - stock\ investment\ percentage$

Stock Investment Amount
$$= total\ investment\ amount * stock\ investment\ percentage$$

Bond Investment Amount
$$= total\ investment\ amount - stock\ investment\ amount$$

Tables

Table 1.1 David's Initial Budget

David's Initial Budget

Fixed Expenses		Wealth-Building		Flexible Expenses	
Rent	$1,000	Monthly Saving	$50	Eating Out	$350
Utilities	$150	Debt payments above minimum	$1500	Entertainment	$150
Car Insurance	$100			Hobbies	$100
Groceries	$150			Gym	$50
Gasoline	$75			Cable TV	$150
Health Insurance	$150			Internet	$75
Minimum Debt Payments	$550			Mobile Phone	$120
				Subscriptions	$50
				Shopping	$200
Total	$2,175	Total	$200	Total	$1,245
% of Income	72.5%	% of Income	6.7%	% of Income	41.5%

Total	$3,620
% of Income	120.7%

Current Savings	$0

Table 1.2 David's Phase 1 Budget

David's Phase 1 Budget

Fixed Expenses		Wealth-Building		Flexible Expenses	
Rent (cheaper apartment)	$600	Saving, Investing, and Paying Debt	$600	Eating Out (more cooking)	$200
Utilities (more efficient use)	$75			Entertainment	$150
Car Insurance (increased deductible)	$75			Hobbies	$100
Groceries (bargain shopping)	$100			Gym	$50
Gasoline (walking/biking)	$50			Cable TV (discontinued)	$0
Health Insurance	$150			Internet	$75
Minimum Debt Payments	$550			Mobile Phone	$120
				Subscriptions	$50
				Shopping (no impulse buys)	$55
Total	$1,600	Total	$600	Total	$800
% of Income	53.3%	% of Income	20.0%	% of Income	26.7%

Total	$3,000
% of Income	100%

Current Savings	$0

Table 2.1 David's Monthly Savings Record

Monthly Savings Record	
David's Initial Savings	$0
Savings After 1 Month	$720
Savings After 2 Months	$1,440

Table 2.2 David's Phase 2 Budget

David's Phase 2 Budget

Fixed Expenses		Wealth-Building		Flexible Expenses	
Rent	$600	Saving, Investing, and Paying Debt	$720	Eating Out	$200
Utilities	$75			Entertainment	$150
Car Insurance	$75			Hobbies	$100
Groceries	$100			Gym	$50
Gasoline	$50			Cable TV	$0
Health Insurance	$150			Internet	$75
Minimum Debt Payments	$550			Mobile Phone	$120
				Subscriptions	$50
				Shopping	$55
Total	$1,600	Total	$720	Total	$800
% of Income	51.3%	% of Income	23.1%	% of Income	25.6%

Total	$3,120
% of Income	100.0%

Current Savings	$1,440

Table 3.1 David's Debt Summary

David's Debt Summary

Debt Name	Amount Owed	Interest Rate	Minimum Payment	Contact Number
Visa	$3,000	18.0%	$75	555-XXX-XXXX
MasterCard	$500	17.5%	$15	555-XXX-XXXX
Macys	$200	15.0%	$5	555-XXX-XXXX
Car Loan	$8,000	5.0%	$250	555-XXX-XXXX
Student Loan	$10,000	4.0%	$205	555-XXX-XXXX
Total	$21,700		$550	

Table 3.2 Consolidated Debt Summary

Consolidated Debt Summary

Debt Name	Amount Owed	Interest Rate	Minimum Payment
Consolidation Loan	$21,700	5%	$430
Visa	$0	18.0%	$0
MasterCard	$0	17.5%	$0
Macys	$0	15.0%	$0
Car Loan	$0	5.0%	$0
Student Loan	$0	4.0%	$0
Total	**$21,700**		**$430**

Table 3.3 Consolidation Final Result

Consolidation Final Results

Months to Pay Off	**18**
Total Interest Paid	**$860**

Table 3.4 Snowball Debt Summary

Snowball Debt Summary

Debt Name	Amount Owed	Minimum Payment
Macys	$200	$5
MasterCard	$500	$15
Visa	$3,000	$75
Car Loan	$8,000	$250
Student Loan	$10,000	$205
Total	**$21,700**	**$550**

Table 3.5 Snowball Month 1 Payment Summary

Snowball Month 1 Payment Summary

Debt Name	Amount Owed	Minimum Payment	Wealth-Building Payment	Total Payment
Macys	$200	$5	$195	$200
MasterCard	$500	$15	$485	$500
Visa	$3,000	$75	$40	$115
Car Loan	$8,000	$250	$0	$250
Student Loan	$10,000	$205	$0	$205
Total	$21,700	$550	$720	$1,270

Table 3.6 Snowball Month 2 Payment Summary

Snowball Month 2 Payment Summary

Debt Name	Amount Owed	Minimum Payment	Wealth-Building Payment	Total Payment
Macys	$0	$0	$0	$0
MasterCard	$0	$0	$0	$0
Visa	$2,885	$75	$740	$815
Car Loan	$7,750	$250	$0	$250
Student Loan	$9,795	$205	$0	$205
Total	$20,430	$530	$740	$1,270

Table 3.7 Snowball Month 3 Payment Summary

Snowball Month 3 Payment Summary

Debt Name	Amount Owed	Minimum Payment	Wealth-Building Payment	Total Payment
Macys	$0	$0	$0	$0
MasterCard	$0	$0	$0	$0
Visa	$2,070	$75	$740	$815
Car Loan	$7,500	$250	$0	$250
Student Loan	$9,590	$205	$0	$205
Total	$19,160	$530	$740	$1,270

Table 3.8 Snowball Final Results

Snowball Final Results	
Months to Pay Off	18
Total Interest Paid	$870

Table 3.9 High Interest First Debt Summary

High Interest First Debt Summary

Debt Name	Amount Owed	Interest Rate
Visa	$3,000	18.0%
MasterCard	$500	17.5%
Macys	$200	15.0%
Car Loan	$8,000	5.0%
Student Loan	$10,000	4.0%
Total	$21,700	

Table 3.10 High Interest First Month 1 Payment Summary

High Interest First Month 1 Payment Summary

Debt Name	Amount Owed	Interest Rate	Minimum Payment	Wealth-Building Payment	Total Payment
Visa	$3,000	18.0%	$75	$720	$795
MasterCard	$500	17.5%	$15	$0	$15
Macys	$200	15.0%	$5	$0	$5
Car Loan	$8,000	5.0%	$250	$0	$250
Student Loan	$10,000	4.0%	$205	$0	$205
Total	$21,700		$550	$720	$1,270

Table 3.11 High Interest First Month 2 Payment Summary

High Interest First Month 2 Payment Summary

Debt Name	Amount Owed	Interest Rate	Minimum Payment	Wealth-Building Payment	Total Payment
Visa	$2,205	18.0%	$75	$720	$795
MasterCard	$485	17.5%	$15	$0	$15
Macys	$195	15.0%	$5	$0	$5
Car Loan	$7,750	5.0%	$250	$0	$250
Student Loan	$9,795	4.0%	$205	$0	$205
Total	$20,430		$550	$720	$1,270

Table 3.12 High Interest First Month 5 Payment Summary

High Interest First Month 5 Payment Summary

Debt Name	Amount Owed	Interest Rate	Minimum Payment	Wealth-Building Payment	Total Payment
Visa	$0	18.0%	$0	$0	$0
MasterCard	$260	17.5%	$15	$245	$260
Macys	$180	15.0%	$5	$175	$180
Car Loan	$7,000	5.0%	$250	$375	$625
Student Loan	$9,180	4.0%	$205	$0	$205
Total	$16,620		$475	$795	$1,270

Table 3.13 High Interest First Final Results

High Interest First Final Results	
Months to Pay Off	18
Total Interest Paid	$865

Table 3.14 David's Phase 3 Budget

David's Phase 3 Budget

Fixed Expenses		Wealth-Building		Flexible Expenses	
Rent	$600	Saving, Investing, and Paying Debt	$1,270	Eating Out	$200
Utilities	$75			Entertainment	$150
Car Insurance	$75			Hobbies	$100
Groceries	$100			Gym	$50
Gasoline	$50			Cable TV	$0
Health Insurance	$150			Internet	$75
Minimum Debt Payments	$0			Mobile Phone	$120
				Subscriptions	$50
				Shopping	$55
Total	$1,050	Total	$1,270	Total	$800
% of Income	33.7%	% of Income	40.7%	% of Income	25.6%

Total	$3,120
% of Income	100%

Current Savings	$1,440

Table 4.1 David's Updated Budget

David's Updated Budget

Fixed Expenses		Wealth-Building		Flexible Expenses	
Rent	$600	Saving, Investing, and Paying Debt	$1,270	Eating Out	$200
Utilities	$75			Entertainment	$150
Car Insurance	$75			Hobbies	$100
Groceries	$100			Gym	$50
Gasoline	$50			Cable TV	$0
Health Insurance	$150			Internet	$75
Minimum Debt Payments	$0			Mobile Phone	$120
				Subscriptions	$50
				Shopping	$55
Total	$1,050	Total	$1,270	Total	$800
% of Income	33.7%	% of Income	40.7%	% of Income	25.6%

Total	$3,120
% of Income	100.0%

Current Savings	$1,440

Table 4.2 Monthly Savings Record

Monthly Savings Record	
David's Initial Savings	$1,440
Savings After 1 Month	$2,710
Savings After 2 Months	$3,980
Savings After 3 Months	$5,250
Savings After 4 Months	$6,520
Savings After 5 Months	$7,790
Savings After 6 Months	$9,060
Savings After 7 Months	$10,330
Savings After 8 Months	$11,600
Savings After 9 Months	$12,870
Savings After 10 Months	$14,140
Savings After 11 Months	$15,410
Savings After 12 Months	$16,680
Savings After 13 Months	$17,950
Savings After 14 Months	$19,220
Savings After 15 Months	$20,490
Savings After 16 Months	$21,760
Savings After 17 Months	**$23,030**

Table 4.3 David's Phase 4 Budget

David's Phase 4 Budget

Fixed Expenses		Wealth-Building		Flexible Expenses	
Rent	$600	Saving, Investing, and Paying Debt	$1,270	Eating Out	$200
Utilities	$75			Entertainment	$150
Car Insurance	$75			Hobbies	$100
Groceries	$100			Gym	$50
Gasoline	$50			Cable TV	$0
Health Insurance	$150			Internet	$75
Minimum Debt Payments	$0			Mobile Phone	$120
				Subscriptions	$50
				Shopping	$55
Total	$1,050	Total	$1,270	Total	$800
% of Income	33.7%	% of Income	40.7%	% of Income	25.6%

Total	$3,120
% of Income	100.0%

Current Savings	$23,030

Table 5.1 David's Updated Budget

David's Updated Budget

Fixed Expenses		Wealth-Building		Flexible Expenses	
Rent	$600	Saving, Investing, and Paying Debt	$1,120	Eating Out	$200
Utilities	$75			Entertainment	$150
Car Insurance	$75			Hobbies	$100
Groceries	$100			Gym	$50
Gasoline	$50			Cable TV (Cable renewed)	$150
Health Insurance	$150			Internet	$75
Minimum Debt Payments	$0			Mobile Phone	$120
				Subscriptions	$50
				Shopping	$55
Total	$1,050	Total	$1,120	Total	$950
% of Income	33.7%	% of Income	35.9%	% of Income	30.4%

Total	$3,120
% of Income	100.0%

Current Savings	$23,030

Table 5.2 David's Phase 5 Budget

David's Phase 5 Budget

Fixed Expenses		Wealth-Building		Flexible Expenses	
Rent	$600	401(k) for company match (10%)	$312	Eating Out	$200
Utilities	$75	Roth IRA	$458	Entertainment	$150
Car Insurance	$75	401(k) Additional contribution	$350	Hobbies	$100
Groceries	$100			Gym	$50
Gasoline	$50			Cable TV	$150
Health Insurance	$150			Internet	$75
Minimum Debt Payments	$0			Mobile Phone	$120
				Subscriptions	$50
				Shopping	$55
Total	$1,050	Total	$1,120	Total	$950
% of Income	33.7%	% of Income	35.9%	% of Income	30.4%

Total	$3,120
% of Income	100.0%

Current Savings	$23,030

Table 6.1 David's Current Budget

David's Current Budget

Fixed Expenses		Wealth-Building		Flexible Expenses	
Rent	$600	401(k)	$662	Eating Out	$200
Utilities	$75	Roth IRA	$458	Entertainment	$150
Car Insurance	$75			Hobbies	$100
Groceries	$100			Gym	$50
Gasoline	$50			Cable TV	$150
Health Insurance	$150			Internet	$75
Minimum Debt Payments	$0			Mobile Phone	$120
				Subscriptions	$50
				Shopping	$55
Total	$1,050	Total	$1,120	Total	$950
% of Income	33.7%	% of Income	35.9%	% of Income	30.4%

Total	$3,120
% of Income	100.0%

Current Savings	$23,030

Table 6.2 David's Final Budget

David's Final Budget

Fixed Expenses		Wealth-Building		Flexible Expenses	
Rent	$600	401(k) Stocks	$536	Eating Out	$200
Utilities	$75	401(k) Bonds	$126	Entertainment	$150
Car Insurance	$75	Roth IRA Stocks	$371	Hobbies	$100
Groceries	$100	Roth IRA Bonds	$87	Gym	$50
Gasoline	$50			Cable TV	$150
Health Insurance	$150			Internet	$75
Minimum Debt Payments	$0			Mobile Phone	$120
				Subscriptions	$50
				Shopping	$55
Total	$1,050	Total	$1,120	Total	$950
% of Income	33.7%	% of Income	35.9%	% of Income	30.4%

Total	$3,120
% of Income	100.0%

Current Savings	$23,030